Table of Contents

Introduction 1

Chapter 1: Why It Doesn't Matter That Age Matters 5

Chapter 2: Playing It Light Is Playing It Right 9

Chapter 3: Where to Prowl and How to Growl 13

Chapter 4: Dressing the Part 21

Chapter 5: Romancing the Younger Man 25

Chapter 6: Shooting for Long Term 29

Chapter 7: Side-Stepping the Pitfalls of Cougar Dating 33

Conclusion 37

Introduction

Just because he's younger than you by a good ten years, or even twenty years, does not mean he can't feel intense attraction for you. Every day and every hour, a young man pines intensely for the affections of a woman many years his senior. When an older woman knows what she's doing, she can powerfully captivate the imagination and desire of younger men just as effectively (or even more so) than much younger women.

Attracting and successfully dating younger men boils down to learning how to flaunt one's assets, develop a sense of mystery, and minimize one's vulnerabilities and insecurities. If you're interested in having fun, you definitely want to read this book. And if you're interested in developing a long term relationship with a younger man, you absolutely **need** to read it.

This book will provide a concise yet thorough step-by-step guide to help you become the fiercest and most fabulous of cougars. Get ready to prowl.

© Copyright 2014 by Miafn LLC - All rights reserved.

This document is geared towards providing reliable information in regards to the topic and issue covered. The publication is sold with the idea that the publisher is not required to render accounting, officially permitted, or otherwise, qualified services. If advice is necessary, legal or professional, a practiced individual in the profession should be ordered.

- From a Declaration of Principles which was accepted and approved equally by a Committee of the American Bar Association and a Committee of Publishers and Associations.

In no way is it legal to reproduce, duplicate, or transmit any part of this document in either electronic means or in printed format. Recording of this publication is strictly prohibited and any storage of this document is not allowed unless with written permission from the publisher. All rights reserved.

The information provided herein is stated to be truthful and consistent, in that any liability, in terms of inattention or otherwise, by any usage or abuse of any policies, processes, or directions contained within is solely and completely the responsibility of the recipient reader. Under no circumstances will any legal responsibility or blame be held against the publisher for any reparation, damages, or monetary loss due to the information herein, either directly or indirectly.

Respective authors own all copyrights not held by the publisher.

The information herein is offered for informational purposes solely, and is universal as so. The presentation of the information is without contract or any type of guarantee assurance.

The trademarks that are used are without any consent, and the publication of the trademark is without permission or backing by the trademark owner. All trademarks and brands within this book are for clarifying purposes only and are the owned by the owners themselves, not affiliated with this document.

Chapter 1: Why It Doesn't Matter That Age Matters

Let's not be unrealistic. If you're serious about being successful with dating younger men, then you need to face facts. And the facts are that being an older woman in the dating game has *some* disadvantages. Mainly two:

1) Younger women, in general, are perceived as being more physically attractive. This is the result of generations of evolutionary programming, though as with many other facets of nature, exceptions to the norm are widespread.

2) Men interested in longer term relationships tend to be more comfortable with a large age spread if the woman is younger and the man older.

Now, keeping our grip on cold reality, let's assess each of these potential obstacles. Regarding physical attractiveness, there are multiple factors that go into a woman's overall level of physical attractiveness: fitness, style, attitude, femininity—just to name a few. And, unlike the age factor, most all other measures of attractiveness are measures which can be controlled and improved upon. If you're able to really dial in these other aspects of physical attractiveness, then the age factor will quickly shrink into the background. At any age, a woman who takes good care of herself is going to be more attractive than a woman who does not.

For older women who are just looking to have fun on the dating scene, the likelihood of finding a successful long-term relationship may not be of the utmost concern. But for older women in search of a longer term Mr. Right, it's important to realize that a twenty-year age gap may seem a bit daunting to the man twenty years your junior. A ten-year spread is a lot more palatable, and it's not uncommon to find couples who are married or in serious long-term relationships where the woman is roughly ten years older than the man. The advantage of being a cougar is that you have the power to enamor, and men who are enamored aren't really all that concerned with what their relationship might look like several years down the road. In romance, men are creatures of the moment. For the rest of this book, we'll focus more so on the here and now of attracting younger men rather than worry too much about what the future may hold. After all, being a cougar is about being free, wild, and passionate in the present moment. Life's too short to worry.

Chapter 2: Playing It Light Is Playing It Right

From this point forward, the world is your playground. You are dating to have fun. If you were dating to find security, then you'd be shacked up on a ranch somewhere helping some codger burn off his IRA. You wouldn't be going after younger men. As an older woman, it's important for you to realize that dating younger men means dating immature men. Women are more mature then men from the get-go, so it follows that older women are veritably light years ahead of younger men when it comes to maturity. Do not expect anything different or you will be setting yourself up for frustration, failure, and possibly heartbreak.

The number one rule of dating younger men is Light is Right, not in the dietary sense (though that helps too), but in terms of one's attitude. The easiest way to make the fact of your age stick out like a sore thumb and detract from your sex appeal is to present yourself as a gravely-serious dater with very serious, well-defined, and perhaps urgent reasons for involving yourself in the dating scene. A cougar is powerful, mysterious, and playful, not desperate, transparent, and glum.

The way of the cougar is playful by way of mystery, not playful by way of ditsy. This is how you turn your age into an asset. Be flirtatious without being

Chapter 3: Where to Prowl and How to Growl

Meeting younger men isn't as difficult as you might think. For starters, any time you go out, it's important that you look and feel sexy. Remember, fitness and style are two factors of attraction that, when properly leveraged, can take the age issue right off the table. Look good, feel good, and have a light and mysterious attitude. Here are some venues where you can find success on your next prowl:

The Supermarket: The mecca of cougar dating, the supermarket is full of hot young stock boys and wandering bachelors who would like nothing more than to spark up some flirtations with a sexy older woman. A simple smile, or perhaps a question, can start a conversation: "Where's the bread aisle?"

Clubs and Meet-ups: What are you interested in? Scuba-diving? Tennis? Politics? Whatever it is, there's probably a meet-up group for it you can join online (www.meetup.com). Would-be cougars can do quite well at physical club activities such as softball and ultimate Frisbee.

College Campus: No, you shouldn't stake out the student center and troll around for younger guys, unless you're exceptionally ambitious. But if you're interested in improving yourself, take a college class or two. You'll get to learn a little and you'll also increase your proximity to a limitless supply of young studs.

Night Clubs: There's really no reason a hot older woman can't live it up until late hours at the club. You may have to dodge a few drunken idiots, but you may also be approached by a young hottie or two who finds your mature debonair sensibilities to be irresistible.

The Shopping Mall: Malls are full of young guys on the hunt. Try sitting on a bench in clear view of the heavy foot traffic. If you've got nice legs, show them off. You're bound to be approached.

The Park: What better way to spend a sunny Sunday afternoon than with a nice prowl through the park. If you're lucky maybe you'll bring back some fresh meat.

Swanky Bars: There's something a bit incongruent about a suave, confident, older woman guzzling cheap beer at a dive bar. But not all bars are created equal. Micro-breweries can often be very classy venues and wholly appropriate haunts for hip and sexy older women. Take a stroll downtown and look for other venues where you'd be comfortable throwing back a few. And go out on a Wednesday or Tuesday night, so you don't get lost in the commotion. There's something positively scintillating about meeting a hot older woman at a quiet classy bar. It's what the best fantasies are made of.

Concerts: What better than music to break down intergenerational barriers? Meeting a guy at concert will automatically give you something in common to talk about.

Online: The most obvious place to meet younger men is on the world wide web. There are a handful of specialty dating websites that cater to cougars and the men interested in dating them. Remember to play up your profile with lots of fun and attractive pictures of the awesomeness that is you.

Regardless of which venue you choose, the most important thing to remember is to keep your hunting spirit alive and healthy. Some people like to say that you tend to meet people when you're not looking. This is rubbish. The truth is that you do often meet people in unexpected ways, but if you're not trying then you're probably not going to have much success. Cultivate the mentality of the hunter. Go out and prowl about and have a good time in the process. Your moment may come at an unexpected time or location, perhaps somewhere not mentioned in the list above, but it will be much more likely to come (and you'll be more prepared for it) if you're taking all possible actions to maximize your chances.

Most men will take the lead if you send them the proper buying signals. Start with a smile. If you need to be a little more aggressive then escalate up to a random question. Young, old, or otherwise: if a guy likes you, he'll take the lead if he thinks you might be interested.

One of the allures of dating or even flirting with an older woman is that they are usually not afraid to be a little more direct. They know what they want and don't play games. As an older woman, it's ok to take the lead at times during the courtship process if need be. For example, inviting a guy out for lunch, for a drink, or to a club activity is fair game for a cougar so long as it doesn't come off as needy. A cougar should have thick skin and should act and speak with confidence. If you're interested in a guy, you're going to let him know, and you will escalate where appropriate. There's nothing wrong with that. If it turns out he's attached or not interested, so be it. It's his loss.

When flirting, you can be bold without being too direct. If you're flirting with a guy who is strikingly attractive on a physical level, you can bring it up subtly and always with an air of sultriness: "You look like you take really good care of yourself." Now, the normal woman would stop here, but in order to assert that you are a bold and beautiful sexual being, hot on the prowl, the cougar might add "If you want, I could take good care of you too." At this point, if he's interested you'll know it. He'll be a little nervous, his pupils might dilate a little bit and if he's got game, he may fire back his own line to advance the banter. If he's not interested, the remark you make can easily be laughed off without anyone having to suffer a bruised ego.

Remember to always keep things light and fun, even if you're nervous. In fact a little nervousness when talking to younger men is a good thing so long as you also evoke an inner confidence. A touch of nervousness can give you just the right amount of vulnerability and damsel-in-distress femininity to balance out your powerful and independent attributes brought out by graceful aging. The best advice, really, is to not think about it too much, try and have fun, and don't act surprised if you get asked out on a date.

During your dates, you need to be yourself. Don't try to dress or act younger than you really are. Also don't feel that you need to pick up the check, even if you make double his salary. Don't anticipate being smarter or wiser than him. Instead, you should be open to learning things from him that you didn't know. This will help to add some healthy balance to the dynamic. Avoid saying things like, "When I was your age," or anything else that sets you apart generationally. Your goal for the date is to connect, not delineate yourselves from one another. It's also very important to maintain your air of independence. Don't try and get him to commit to another date right there on the spot. If he likes you, he will pursue you. Avoid the subject of commitment or exclusivity for at least the first several months of dating. If he brings up the subject and it's something that *you're* interested in, fine, but for your part, strive to keep things as light as possible.

Chapter 4: Dressing the Part

As is true with so many other aspects of dating younger men, the most important key to dressing attractively is learning to play to your strengths. An older woman is going to look her best when she dresses in a way that's classy and elegant. If you're not twenty-one, then don't try to dress like a twenty-one year old would dress. No need for skin tight mini-skirts and six-inch heels. Instead try a sexy leather skirt and dark boots. Dark colors tend to work nicely on older women overall.

For makeup, think elegant. A lot of older women try to use make up to cover up their age when they should be using it to accentuate their best features. If your makeup is caked on by the pound you risk turning guys off by looking like you're desperate and trying too hard. Your goal should be to look like an attractive and confident older woman and your makeup should be employed to this end. Focus on smooth and light application and use eye shadow, mascara, and lipstick for subtle and elegant highlights. Smell is the great equalizer when it comes to female cosmetics. If you smell sexy, men will have no choice but to be attracted to you.

When it comes to dressing, your years of experience should put you at an advantage over younger women. You should be very comfortable and knowledgeable about your own body. You should know what looks good on you and what you can't pull off. An older woman should wear her clothes with comfort and confidence. She should not be fidgety or self-conscious. Exploit the experience advantage for all it's worth. Be the sexiest, classiest woman on the scene, and the young guys will be turning their heads.

Chapter 5: Romancing the Younger Man

One of the most satisfying aspects of dating younger men is being pleasantly surprised by how fulfilling of a romance a younger man can offer. And this extends well beyond just the bedroom. Younger men are from a different generation and the way they view women is going to be different from the way men from your own generation view women. Many younger men come from homes where their mothers were the sole or equal breadwinners for the family. They will be more inclined to be supportive of your dreams and ambitions and less inclined to be dismissive of them. Rather than viewing women as eternal helpers, they will be more likely to appreciate your sense of power and self-determination. A younger man can provide a very satisfying romance or relationship for a woman who has lofty aspirations for herself professionally or personally. If you want to open your own business or hike the Appalachian Trail, a younger man is more likely to encourage you to take real action on these ambitions rather than steer you towards a stable, work-a-day lifestyle.

There may be some palpable generational gaps. For example, the two of you will likely have differing tastes in music and in other artistic media. But these factors really shouldn't put a damper on the relationship.

The most challenging hardship for dating a younger man will be issues that stem from disparate maturity. If you're dating a man in his twenties, then don't expect him to want to settle down any time soon. Men at this age are often trying to maximize their experience by dating a lot of different women and a so-called "cougar" may very well be their next fleeting fancy. It's important to be realistic in this regard and manage your expectations appropriately.

In his late twenties, a man will have more knowledge about what he wants in a relationship. He will also likely have had some success in his career and will thus be a little more stable. By his early to mid-thirties, a man will probably have even had his heart broken a time or two and will begin to understand his values in a relationship and what he needs and wants long-term. Don't count your chickens though, a lot of men remain serial daters well into their forties—another byproduct of generational differences.

Though the role of the sexually-experienced cougar may be prevalent in pop culture, it is not necessarily factual. The younger generations, thanks in large part to the internet, have grown up in an environment where sex is much less taboo.

Young men especially tend to be exposed to pornography very early in life and are often sexually active in their early teens. The attitude towards sex among the younger generation is much more casual.

Don't be surprised if your younger man has more bedroom experience than you.

The best approach to relating to a younger man is similar to the approach you will use when attracting him—play up the positives. Dating a younger man is an opportunity to be adventurous and spontaneous, to expose yourself to new views of the world and possibly yourself. Pack up and go to India for a few months. Go skydiving. Open a bakery or audition for a role in a movie. Remember you're not in this for security; you're in this to feel alive.

Chapter 6: Shooting for Long Term

If the young guy you're dating makes you feel appreciated, excited, and happy overall, then maybe he's a keeper. If, by contrast, he makes you feel your age, if he's difficult to relate to, or if you're otherwise incompatible, then it's certainly ok to move on, regardless of how old you are. Don't ever settle for something that doesn't work just so you don't have to be alone.

If you're thinking you might have a long-term relationship on your hands, then start having some conversations about longer term issues. You should be aware of and forthcoming about your ability and desire to have children. If you are too old to have children, then you should talk about the possibility of adopting.

When it comes to families, regardless of the age difference, if the two of you truly make one another happy, then your respective families should acknowledge this and support the progress and development of your relationship. It's important that you don't treat your partner like a show-dog—don't try and show off to your family or anyone for that matter that you're dating a younger man. And if projecting an image for yourself of youth and vitality is a primary reason for your continued dating of a younger man, then definitely don't proceed with creating a longer term commitment. Instead, ask yourself honestly if you're ready to spend the rest of your life with this man.

If you decide that you do indeed want to pursue a longer term relationship, or even the prospect of marriage, then you'll need to think about the different spheres of responsibility in the relationship. Since you're older, you may be making quite a bit more money than him, so you may find yourself to be the primary breadwinner of your pending committed relationship or marriage. Therefore, it's important to recognize and encourage some other important area where your younger husband-to-be can contribute. Otherwise you risk an inappropriately lopsided dynamic that will end with you feeling drained and used and him feeling unfulfilled and helpless.

If you do plan to have a child or to adopt, then there's nothing wrong with having the man oversee daily childcare and other domestic duties. It's also perfectly acceptable for both of you to continue to focus on your careers and not have children. Even if he's making less money than you, if he has a fulfilling job and has you to lean on for encouragement and support, then the two of you have the framework for a very healthy and prosperous partnership. It may also be a good idea at this point to think about retirement realities. Are you putting enough away into retirement to continue to support the families quality of life after you retire? Is your husband-to-be okay with the possibility of having to take care of you in your old age, when he's perhaps only 50 or 60 years old?

The realities of highly age-disparate couples may present some challenging situations to consider, but in the end if the two of you are happy being together as a couple and wish to continue as such, you shouldn't let age get in the way.

Chapter 7: Side-Stepping the Pitfalls of Cougar Dating

For a woman to have success dating a younger man, she must exert expert control over her ego. Too many women quickly fall too far into the role of sole decision maker, know-it-all, or worse, mother. Dating and relationships are a two-way street, regardless of age differences. It's important that you strive to make your partner feel important and secure.

There will inevitably be times when he shows his age in a way that's not very flattering. Whether it's a naïve opinion or a shortfall of maturity, there will be times when you're tempted to criticize him under the warrant of being older and knowing more. Don't give in to this temptation. Find other ways to introduce him to your wisdom by showing him by example that your ideas are about sophistication, manners, class, and respect. If he appreciates and admires you as he should, then he'll take your example to heart.

Learn to appreciate him for all the unique and insightful things he brings to the relationship. Even if his only strong suit is high competencies in the use of Twitter and Instagram, look for things that you can learn from his unique generational experience and don't discount them.

Unfortunately, a lot of younger men with low self-esteem will regress into very dependent roles when dating an older woman and this can lead to disaster. You date someone so you can be their girlfriend, not their mother. Here are a few things you can do to prevent this type of regression:

Don't Be Anyone's Sugar Momma

There's nothing wrong with a woman picking up the check from time to time. If you are an accomplished female of independent means, then you should be proud and feel free to flaunt your purchasing power. Just don't do it too much. If you're dating a younger man, the age spread makes it easier for you to slide into the role of constant financier. The key word of concern in "Sugar Momma" is "Momma." In a romantic partnership, it's important to let your man play the part of the "man" by letting him be a provider and procurer, even if his income is a piddling fraction of your own. As a good rule of thumb—try and avoid the unemployed types.

Avoid Younger Men with Drug or Alcohol Dependency Issues

Men who struggle with issues of addiction should never be at the top of your "to-date" list, and especially so if you are dating younger men. If you're older, wealthier, and more experienced with life, a younger man with a drinking or drug problem will find countless avenues to suck you dry. From classic addict behaviors, such as borrowing money that he never intends to return, to frequent emotional outbursts, your role will quickly transform from girlfriend to both mother and therapist. And no matter how nice he is to look at, after dealing with an addict for a few months you'll get to a point where even looking at him fills you with dread and disgust.

Avoid Low Self-Esteem Cases

Even if he's not jonesing for his next fix of heroin, dating a younger guy with terrible self-esteem is going to make for a terrible relationship. He will constantly depend on you to validate him since he can't do it on his own. He will prove helpless in the face of any new challenge and become accustomed to you taking charge in all trying situations. Your roll will be that of a mother mixed with a cheerleader, which does not make for a happy hybrid.

The best cougar matches are with young men who have a good sense of discipline, pride, and self-worth. Go after guys who are self-starters, young entrepreneurs, or artists who are passionate about life. Look for young men who are involved in hobbies and communities, who take their grandmothers to church, and volunteer to serve the poor. Make sure he's worthy of you.

Conclusion

The overarching principle of dating younger men is playing up your strengths and accepting — not hiding — your weaknesses. Men are biologically programmed to want younger women because the instinct-driven part of their brains tells them that a younger woman has the best chance of producing healthy offspring. There's nothing anyone can do to change the biological basis of attraction, but you can and should play up the exoticism of being an older woman. You do this by being confident and mysterious, bold yet feminine, and by always being on the hunt.

Finally, I'd like to thank you for purchasing this book! If you enjoyed it or found it helpful, I'd greatly appreciate it if you'd take a moment to leave a review on Amazon. Thank you!

Printed in Great Britain
by Amazon

Cougar Dating

The Secrets to Success for Older Women Dating Younger Men

by Jackson Sparks